ESSENTIAL MANAGERS

FLEXIBLE WORKING

Produced for DK by Dynamo Ltd
1 Cathedral Court, Southernhay East, Exeter, EX1 1AF

Written by Lara Kavanagh and Wes Nicholson
Senior Art Editor Helen Spencer
Senior Editor Chauney Dunford
Jacket Design Development Manager Sophia MTT
Jacket Designer Akiko Kato
Producer Rachel Ng
Production Editor Gillian Reid
Senior Managing Art Editor Lee Griffiths
Managing Editor Gareth Jones
Associate Publishing Director Liz Wheeler
Art Director Karen Self
Design Director Philip Ormerod
Publishing Director Jonathan Metcalf

First published in Great Britain in 2021 by Dorling Kindersley Limited
DK, One Embassy Gardens, 8 Viaduct Gardens, London, SW11 7BW

The authorised representative in the EEA is Dorling Kindersley Verlag GmbH.
Arnulfstr. 124, 80636 Munich, Germany

Copyright © 2021 Dorling Kindersley Limited
A Penguin Random House Company
10 9 8 7 6 5 4 3 2 1
001-325012-May/2021

A CIP catalogue record for this book
is available from the British Library.
ISBN: 978-0-2415-1564-8

Printed and bound in the UK

For the curious
www.dk.com

MIX
Paper from
responsible sources
FSC™ C018179

This book was made with Forest
Stewardship Council ™ certified paper
- one small step in DK's commitment
to a sustainable future. For more
information go to www.dk.com/our-
green-pledge

FLEXIBLE
WORKING

Contents

Introduction

Technological strides have changed the landscape of work dramatically. Empowered by improved connectivity and a better understanding of workers' needs, more organizations than ever are offering flexible working conditions, including job shares, home-working, and part-time hours. These all present new challenges for managers. You can now cast your hiring net all over the world, giving recruits the freedom to pick where they live while accessing the professional opportunities they want. Tools such as video conferencing reduce the need to travel, help to avoid the need for a daily commute, and free up office space for staff whose jobs cannot be done remotely.

As the Covid-19 pandemic taught managers the world over, remote working is not just possible, but highly effective when organized well. Research shows that employee productivity is often higher and stress levels lower. As a manager looking to nurture contented, productive employees, you will need to understand the trickier aspects of remote working, as well as the specific needs of your staff. Importantly, you and any of your employees based in their own living spaces must learn how to strike a balance that ensures working from home doesn't feel like living at work.

Flexible Working is a clear guide for managers working remotely, managing distributed colleagues, coordinating hybrid teams, or transitioning to remote work from a shared office. Offering expert advice, tips, and case studies, it will help you tackle the challenges and reap the benefits of remote working. You will learn how to set yourself and others up for success, choosing the right tools for online collaboration, adopting virtual etiquette, and developing the leadership skills you need to get the best out of staff who don't share a physical work space.

Working
remotely

Remote working requires a different approach to operating in a shared space. You need to learn how to organize your days, stay motivated, and achieve a healthy balance between your professional and home life. As a manager, the example you set will inspire other colleagues to excel from afar.

01

Rethinking the office

Around the world, managers are taking a more flexible approach to how and where their staff work. Tech advances are enabling effective remote collaboration and many leaders are seeing the benefits in terms of better focused and happier employees. Do you still need a shared office at all?

Increasing productivity

While some organizations still need staff to collaborate in person, most are now unlikely to insist on everyone working in the same physical space all the time. Even before the Covid-19 pandemic struck, many businesses embraced the benefits of letting staff work remotely where possible. Adopting home-working days frees up room in work spaces and gives staff time to concentrate on tasks with fewer distractions. It also saves them commuting time, helping to achieve a healthier work/life balance. Any employers sceptical about long-term home working for employees should note that in 2019, 85 per cent of businesses reported increases in productivity after introducing flexible working. So, you can argue that the traditional shared work space is no longer needed in some fields. But whether at home, in a co-working setup, at company premises, or in a combination of locations, staff still need a suitable space with the right technology in place for them to function.

Personal connections

Better meeting technology allows you to stay in "face-to-face" contact with your colleagues. Remote working does not have to be impersonal.

50%

of employees work outside of their main office for at least **two-and-a-half days a week**

THE DAY HOME WORKING WENT VIRAL

Professor Robert Kelly and his family became internet sensations in 2017 when his children burst in on a live TV interview. Sitting in jacket and tie in his home office in Busan, South Korea, the political analyst looked mortified. But he later gave a cheerful interview alongside his family about the realities of working at home. Fast-forward to the 2020 pandemic, and the difficulties faced by workers balancing professional and home lives during lockdown resulted in several similar interviews. Such incidents highlight the demands on today's employees that can disrupt home-working and their ability to stick to the traditional nine-to-five.

Global talent

Remote working gives you the chance to recruit talent anywhere in the world – not just people within commuting distance of your HQ – and to build a global team.

Digital tools

Cloud storage and collaborative software mean you and your employees can access what they need and work effectively as a team, wherever they are.

Clever communications

As a manager, you have many ways to interact with your staff remotely and get everyone collaborating. These include messaging apps, email, video conferencing, and intranets.

Setting goals

When it comes to setting goals, start with your own. Does working remotely change the way you approach them? Armed with a clear plan for yourself, you can work with each member of your team to create goals that challenge and motivate.

Leading by example

Whether you manage staff who work remotely, or it is you who works in a different location from them, set the standard for effective working by deciding a clear structure for your day. Create a weekly list of priority tasks to slot into that structure to help you reach your personal goals. Encourage team members to do the same, bearing in mind their day needn't look exactly like yours. They can still hit their goals when working flexible hours and terms.

> **Clarity is key** when it comes to setting goals. Make sure **everyone understands** exactly what's expected of them

Creating SMART goals when working remotely

To be effective, each goal you set should be SMART: Specific, Measurable, Achievable, Relevant, and Time-bound. When working remotely, you may need to adapt the scope of each SMART goal and be more diligent with progress checks.

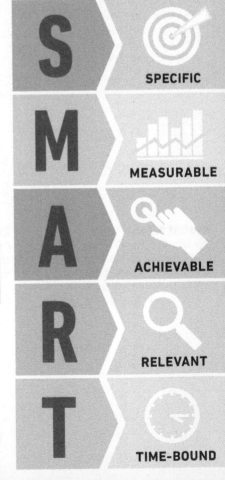

S SPECIFIC

M MEASURABLE

A ACHIEVABLE

R RELEVANT

T TIME-BOUND

Monitoring progress

Report back frequently on your progress to your own manager, highlighting any problems you're facing as soon as they arise. Book one-to-one catch-ups with those who report directly to you to review goal progress, and be ready to adapt if you need to.

Set goals with specific parameters – who, what, where, when, and why. **Record everything** in an online tool (such as Workday) that allows team members to access relevant information wherever they are.

Make your goals measurable by linking them to a quantity – number of sales, for example. With remote teams, think about **breaking goals down** into smaller ones to minimize the risk of slipping off schedule.

Goals should challenge, but never set people up to fail. Does the person in question have all the resources they need to achieve this goal remotely? **Add extra contingency time** for each one, just in case.

From a distance, people can lose a sense of where their work fits into the wider business. **Align every goal** with the strategic goals of the organization, showing each person how their job is relevant to the company as a whole.

Deadlines are not only motivating, but rewarding once you meet them. **Set a firm end date** and book in regular checkpoints. Avoid open time frames, especially for staff new to working remotely and dealing with lots of change.

Staying positive

Working remotely might leave you feeling that your efforts are going unnoticed, and it's the same for your staff. Maintain good contact with your team, taking time to celebrate individual and group successes. This could be via a quick wrap-up video call to share positive feedback on achieved goals, or a reward system (vouchers or a bottle of wine, for instance). Recognizing people's efforts inspires goodwill, improves how people view your management skills, and helps employees working apart from colleagues feel less isolated.

In focus

KEEPING FOCUSED

Loss of focus happens wherever you're working, and always results in decreased productivity. When managing staff remotely, you need to strike a balance between giving people space to perform tasks in peace, while also ensuring work is completed as required.

- Use meetings efficiently – plan them well, get to the point, and make sure everyone has time to complete any related tasks.
- Encourage staff to check emails regularly, but not obsessively – turning off notifications for an hour can boost concentration.
- Keep your written communications clear and to the point, helping others to focus on the task in hand.

Working with others

To be an effective remote manager, you need to understand your staff and colleagues. Get to know people properly, and foster a culture of respect for their individual circumstances, personalities, and working styles.

Collaborating at a distance

When you don't share a work space, you can't pick up on many of the visual cues that people use when communicating – or give them out yourself. This means your interpersonal skills need to come to the fore. Take time to find out about your staff through individual catch-ups, listening carefully, communicating clearly, and showing empathy. This will help you to collaborate successfully, even if you never meet in person.

Communicating well

Stay in regular touch with your team, but bear in mind that video calls can be uncomfortable and anxiety-inducing for some people. Messaging apps such as Slack (see pp.34–35) are good for getting quick answers, but a phone call can be more personal if you need to elaborate on an issue or gauge a mood. If you're not sure what's best, ask the individual how they would prefer to talk.

This call is **overrunning** again, but I have to collect my kids

She knows I'm **hard of hearing**, but she won't stop **calling** for updates

I blocked my **lunch hour** in the calendar, but my manager wants a **meeting**

He's forgotten I'm **part-time** and given me an **impossible deadline**

Respecting personal circumstances

Everyone needs a bit of extra support and understanding from their manager at some point. If a staff member reveals they have a health condition, find out what they need to get their work done without cost to their wellbeing. Consider what it might be like for colleagues who live and work alone – do they need additional support from you? Recognize that some people have caring duties for others that put extra pressure on their time. (Note mothers often have the most limited working hours, and workloads don't always shrink to fit.) By working on an individual level, you can come up with flexible solutions to help everyone stay on track.

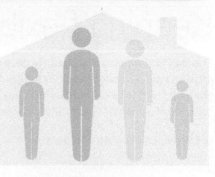

The **more contact** individuals have **with their manager**, the better they feel and **more committed** they are to their health

ASK YOURSELF...
Am I an inclusive manager?

		YES	NO
1	Do I use **simple language** that everyone will understand?	☐	☐
2	Do I consider if I'm talking to someone in their **second language**?	☐	☐
3	Do I take time to find out about **the other person's culture** and any related preferences?	☐	☐
4	Do I offer to **switch to video** so others can **lip read**?	☐	☐
5	Do I take **differing schedules** and personal circumstances into account when I book a meeting?	☐	☐
6	Do I invite **every voice** to be heard?	☐	☐
7	Do I pay attention to **the timing of calls and time zones** when scheduling a meeting with international team members?	☐	☐

Keeping flexible

The best managers are both flexible enough to accommodate differences and capable of adapting to change. In a remote environment, you need to come up with practical solutions to individual scenarios, striking a balance that works for all.

Understanding difference

Your employees don't need to work identically to perform well. Offering flexible working conditions gives you access to a broader range of talents, reflects well on your business, and enhances your reputation as a manager. Once you understand the individual circumstances and requirements of your team members, you can define hours and terms that work for them, without affecting their workload.

Finding time to connect

It can be helpful to overlap as a team for a few hours a day. But if a member is on the other side of the world, or works completely different hours, you will have to come up with other ways to connect. This could be a short bi-weekly virtual meeting or a daily handover email. Occasionally asking someone to join a meeting outside of their agreed hours is fine, but don't make it the norm.

Adapting old habits

THINK BEFORE YOU BOOK

Do you really need that meeting? If you do, does everyone on the team have to be there? Get in the habit of booking shorter slots with carefully considered attendees, minimizing disruption for yourself and others.

BE OPEN TO NEW TECHNOLOGY

Review your existing communication technology and software. Search online and seek recommendations for alternative options that are accessible, simple to use, and affordable.

GIVE PROMPT FEEDBACK

Managers can hold up progress if they don't provide feedback. Respond promptly, so everyone can perfect their projects and move on. If someone has done a particularly good job, tell them – this is especially important for those feeling isolated. When giving negative feedback, be polite, honest, and ready to provide support.

Learning to let go

If you're new to remote working, you may notice a tendency in yourself to micromanage. This shows a lack of trust and can cause frustration. When you're delegating and can't oversee a task in person, keep in regular contact to stay up-to-date, and offer support, but avoid excessive monitoring. Remember that delegating not only helps you balance your own workload, but broadens the professional experience of your staff, priming them for career progression.

Tip

SHARE YOUR SCHEDULE
Work calendars are powerful tools for remote working. Use one to let people know **when you are or aren't available**. Make sure everyone in the team does the same (see pp.54–55).

Balancing work and life

Working remotely brings many benefits for work-life balance. But it can also erode boundaries between your job and your personal time, compelling you to put in more hours and be on call around the clock. Be firm with yourself and others about maintaining a healthy equilibrium.

Setting boundaries

Working more intensely over busy periods is fine, but don't let work stress take over. When you're working remotely, you often feel obliged to do more, especially if you're at home. Set boundaries and share them with your colleagues. Some examples:

- Don't check work messages after hours.
- Respect your own and others' flexible working arrangements.
- Take leave when you need it and encourage others to do the same.
- Put away your work things at the end of the day.
- Move away from your work area when you make personal calls or catch up with a family member.

> **Tip**
>
> **FIND YOUR POWER HOUR**
> Work out **when you're at your best** during the workday and schedule your trickier tasks for that period. You will find you **move through your to-do list** much more efficiently, making it more likely you wrap up on time at the end of each day.

Case study

MAKING BALANCE A PRIORITY

In 2020, Nationwide Building Society brought in a series of new measures to help its remote staff find a healthy work-life balance. The society encouraged employees to use their calendars to re-create some of the structure they had lost after switching from office life to home working. It suggested blocking out virtual commuting time, organizing daily team calls for social catch-ups, and instituted a no-meetings rule over the lunch hour. It also encouraged employees to be more proactive about looking after themselves by providing free company-wide access to Unmind, a mental health platform full of practical information designed to help people monitor and improve their wellbeing.

CHECKLIST...

Achieving balance in your life   **YES   NO**

1 Do I often have **time for my hobbies** outside of work? ☐ ☐

2 Do I have a **regular exercise routine**? ☐ ☐

3 Do I usually get **a good night's sleep**? ☐ ☐

4 Do I have **enough energy** to get me through the day? ☐ ☐

5 Do I **express my feelings**? ☐ ☐

6 Do I have a **clear sense of purpose** in both my personal and work life? ☐ ☐

7 Do I make a **real contribution** at work? ☐ ☐

8 Do I know **who I am and am I happy** with that? ☐ ☐

9 Do I have the chance to **relax properly** after work? ☐ ☐

Structuring your time

Working remotely brings new distractions and disruption, so it's important to have a sensible structure for each day. Things run more smoothly when you have a plan. Start when you say you will, give tasks the attention they deserve, remember to take breaks – and finish on time.

Planning your day

As a manager, you must be available to your team, but you must also reserve time and energy for yourself. Each day write a list of the tasks you need to achieve, both work-related and personal (team meeting, review Project A, call plumber), and refer to it often. Plan in breaks and stress-busting activities, too. Time-management coach Elizabeth Grace Saunders recommends using what she calls a "time budget". Start out by calculating how many hours you have to "spend" each week in order to get a clear sense of what you can reasonably handle. Estimate how long each item on your list will take and note it down – that will show you how achievable your plan is. If it's too much, simply adjust to fit.

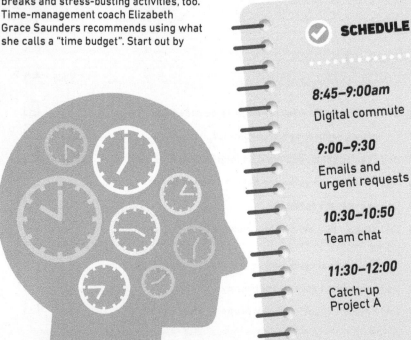

✅ SCHEDULE

8:45–9:00am
Digital commute

9:00–9:30
Emails and urgent requests

10:30–10:50
Team chat

11:30–12:00
Catch-up Project A

Using your calendar

Your daily task list is just for you, but your online calendar is for everyone you work with. Use it to clearly show when you're available to collaborate. Block out times when you need to work uninterrupted and use the period you would have spent travelling to work to draw a distinct line between personal and work time. Enjoy this "digital commute" however you like: 10 minutes listening to your favourite music, a quick stroll, a five-minute meditation – whatever prepares you for the day and helps you wind down again.

In focus

REDUCING STRESS

There are lots of things you can do to lower stress levels while working remotely. Start by muting email notifications when you need to concentrate. Set reminders to take screen breaks, eat your lunch, or simply get out of your chair and stretch. Use your break times to walk, turn on your mindfulness app, or simply take some deep breaths. Now and again, suggest a work social, such as a virtual team meal. Hold this at the end of the day so you can catch up informally over an early dinner. Without a train to catch or traffic to beat, it's easy to let a task drag on past your official hours. Be strict with yourself about wrapping up as planned, turning everything off, and closing the door (literally, if possible) on work.

12:00–1:00pm
Lunch

2:00–2:30
1:1 with Rachel

3:00–3:30
School run

3:30–4:30
Prep for coaching session

5:30–5:45
Digital commute

Learn to **say "no"** when you need to. It shuts down **unreasonable requests** and stops you heading down the path to **burnout**

Looking after mind and body

Some people love the autonomy and peace of working away from their colleagues. Others struggle with the lack of contact. As a remote manager, you need to look after your own mental health and wellbeing, and to watch out for that of others.

Maintaining a connection

When you're not working face to face, it can be hard to feel connected to colleagues, which can impact your mental health for the worse. Maintaining a positive bond with your team will buoy your resilience and confidence, making you a stronger leader. If you're struggling, seek the support of your manager, or a trusted colleague or friend.

In terms of the people you manage, keep in regular virtual contact with them (both as a group and individually) and try to make yourself approachable. Doing your utmost to maintain a happy, supported team will help their focus, their ability to meet deadlines, and also their general outlook. This in turn will make your life own easier and reduce your stress.

ASK YOURSELF...
Is my wellbeing suffering?

	YES	NO
1 Am I **unusually forgetful?**	☐	☐
2 Am I feeling **irritable or lethargic?**	☐	☐
3 Do I feel **worried or tired all the time?**	☐	☐
4 Am I suffering from **regular headaches?**	☐	☐
5 Do I feel **overwhelmed?**	☐	☐
6 Do I have **persistent body aches and pains?**	☐	☐
7 Have I gained or lost a **significant amount of weight recently?**	☐	☐

Encouraging good health

Think about introducing ideas that promote everyone's health and wellbeing. For example, you might start a healthy-eating programme or arrange a delivery of nutritious snack parcels; provide subscriptions to mindfulness apps; or encourage initiatives to build exercise into the workday. You should also champion the importance of regular screen breaks and proper lunch hours for all.

Tip

BE SUPPORTIVE

If you need to provide **emotional support** to a colleague, ask them how they would prefer to talk – by video, phone, or in person if appropriate. Reassure them that any **conversations will remain private**. Listen fully, repeat back the details, and **be positive about finding solutions** to the problem.

Chatting socially

If you or your colleagues find aspects of remote working stressful or lonely, consider introducing a daily or weekly social video call. The only rule? You can't talk about your job. It might sound like a distraction from work tasks, but a 15–30-minute non-work chat can have the opposite effect, providing a moment of human connection that leaves you refreshed and ready to tackle the day.

Understanding personalities

Getting your team working fluidly together is about more than meshing skill sets, it's about managing personalities. The process of understanding people's characters is different when remote working but no less vital. At the same time, be sure not to neglect yourself.

Assessing personality

When asked to describe their characters, people often describe themselves as "introverts" or "extroverts". In a remote setting where people can't interact in person, these traits can be more pronounced: extroverts may become more forceful in their opinions, while introverts may grow more reticent.

Your role isn't to label personalities, but to understand and work with them. When teams meet, personalities affect one other. Quieter members feel intimidated by colleagues who won't stop talking, while those who thrive on thinking out loud get frustrated by those who prefer their own space. Your goal is to get everyone working well together.

Should I say something?

Hmm, I'm not sure that's right

No, I'm sure they've already thought of it

> **Tip**
>
> **LEAVE EGOS AT THE DOOR**
> Every opinion is valid but **"scoring points"** against one another just hurts the team. Professionalism means being able to work with others to achieve a shared goal, so talk to your staff about leaving egos at the door – **your own included**.

In focus

IMPOSTOR SYNDROME?

If you've ever felt out of your depth, you're not alone. "Impostor syndrome" was first identified in an influential 1970s study that estimated that up to 70 per cent of people will at some point question their ability to do what's expected of them professionally. In 2018, former US First Lady Michelle Obama told an audience in London that she still experiences impostor syndrome. The syndrome has no clear cause. Theories range from perfectionism, to personality traits such as anxiety, and early formative experiences of "not being good enough". More important is to understand that it's a normal response that can affect anyone, at any level, in any profession. If you think you might be experiencing impostor syndrome, talk to colleagues and friends, and get your fears out in the open. They can help you reframe your thoughts, and focus on your positive qualities. You might even discover they have had similar experiences.

Managing interactions

When your employees are working apart from each other, you need to spend more time making sure everyone is on the same track. That means more time in meetings, where personalities soon become apparent. You may need to rein in more vociferous colleagues, or encourage quieter ones to contribute. You can discuss how individuals like to work in one-on-one chats. You will want to support those who feel uncomfortable speaking up, but be aware that not everyone reacts well to being forced out of their "comfort zone". Let people know they can raise issues privately for you to address with the group later.

That's a really good point, thanks for raising it

Before we go into that, let's hear Asif's take on this

Running a business

When you run your own company, there's no senior manager to turn to. And in very small businesses, there are often no colleagues, either. To manage yourself and your firm well, you need to stay organized, create the right working environment, and know when to switch off.

Being a savvy self-manager

Much of the advice covered so far in this chapter applies just the same as if you run a small business remotely. For example, it's equally important to look after your mental health and wellbeing, to stay in regular touch with any staff or clients, and to establish clear boundaries between your work and home life. But as a small business owner, you're also likely to be juggling an even greater variety of tasks, from managing staff, to dealing with tax, and pitching for business. To stay on top of everything without getting overwhelmed, follow a plan for each day. Start on time, be strict about taking breaks, and work through a realistic to-do list in priority order. Set a time frame for each item, and record everything you achieve as you go to monitor your progress.

> **Tip**
>
> **USE YOUR FREEDOM**
> Run your own firm? Don't forget **you're your own boss**. While you want to succeed, you also have more freedom to **create a healthy work-life balance** than an employee manager.

If you're still largely **working on paper**, consider moving things such as accountancy and company **documents online**. It saves on physical storage and allows you to **access everything** wherever you are

Creating your work space

Whether you're a freelancer with a laptop or a hands-on maker with a workshop, take time to create a suitable working environment with all the tech and tools (such as stationery) you need. Ensure your work space looks and feels separate to your home life, and make it comfortable, even if it's just a desk and chair in an alcove. Opt for ergonomic equipment, make sure you have enough light and heat, and keep it tidy. Put something in your eye line that motivates you, such as a photo or inspiring quote. As a manager/business owner, you may also be responsible for the physical welfare of staff working remotely, so check your obligations.

55%

of **remote workers** report new **back pain** after starting to work from home

Outsourcing tasks

You can save much-needed energy by outsourcing certain tasks. If there's an activity that isn't best suited to your skills but takes up a lot of time and effort, it can be well worth paying someone else to do it. Think about getting help with:

O PR
O Marketing
O Social media management
O Payroll
O Answering customer calls
O Finding new business leads
O Processing orders
O Bookkeeping and accounting
O HR (if you employ others)
O Secretarial support

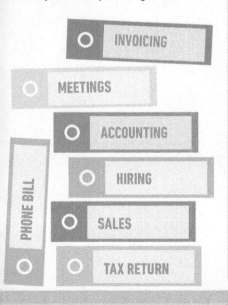

Choosing the
right tools

Managing remotely requires you to use more technology.
That means not only adopting new tools, but also mastering
them. As well as getting to grips with video calls, you need
to understand the pros and cons of different communication
forms, how to collaborate with colleagues effectively at
a distance, and how to keep data safe as you do so.

02

Embracing technology

Switching to remote working means adopting digital technologies – from video-chat tools to online calendars. While some members of your team will relish trying every novel piece of kit, others will be less keen. Your job is to make sure everyone moves forward together.

Understanding what you have

The first step to getting to grips with your remote-working technology is to be clear about everything you have. This isn't about being an expert, but about understanding how and why each system works for you and your team. Conduct an audit of the technology you're using to know whether it's fit for purpose and is suitable for your remote setup. If you're in a position to call on a tech-support consultant, ask them to show you how to use any new systems your organization adopts.

Supporting your team

It doesn't matter that you're quick to adopt technology or have already had the training you need (see pp.84–85) – your team needs to be up to speed, too. According to one survey, 90 per cent of top executives believe their company pays attention to employee needs around new technology, but only 53 per cent of staff think the same. If people are reluctant to embrace new technology, forcing it through won't help. Your team likely comprises a mix of those who love technology and those who recoil from it. Listen to everyone's ideas and concerns to help you all move forward together.

Technology by itself doesn't make leaders. Technology **only amplifies** true leadership

Interact

If you're moving to a remote-working model, your team is likely to face a **barrage of new technology**. They will need to learn at least one meeting platform, and some will need time to adapt. Check in with them, **be patient, and reassure** them that it's a learning experience for everyone.

Invest

Building digital skills is a sound investment, but if your situation is changing rapidly, you may not have the luxury of time. **Share the burden** by deploying the more tech-savvy members of your team as **mentors** to help others get to grips with new tools.

Involve

Introduce digital technologies at a comfortable pace and **involve your team from the start**. If people are left out of the implementation stages, it's harder to get them on board later. Even if you need to act fast, you can still **ask them for feedback** to help you understand what works.

Setting up your office

Working outside of the office means taking responsibility for your own work space. With no HR or IT staff on site to guide you, not only are you often in charge of supplying and maintaining your own office furniture and internet connection, but also managing your health and safety.

Getting the right tools

The first question you need to ask when setting up a remote office is: who is providing the tools? Many organizations give their employees a laptop with the software they need pre-installed, but if yours doesn't, or you're a freelancer using your own equipment, you need to work out what systems you need. Most remote workers require a video-call platform, access to file-sharing services, and other tools that allow team members to collaborate at a distance. They may also require software specific to their roles or unique to your business.

Taking care of yourself

When you work remotely, it is your responsibility to ensure that your work station is safe and fit for purpose. If you work at a computer for long periods, refer to an online guide to make sure you are sitting in front of it correctly in order to prevent eye and muscle strain. For other types of work station, such as a workbench or mobile office, take similar professional advice.

Keeping moving

Take regular breaks to avoid injury when working from home. Being in one position for too long can lead to back, shoulder, or arm pain, so stand up, stretch, and walk around – just don't stay still.

CHECKLIST
Equipping your remote office **YES NO**

Essentials

1 A comfortable desk and chair .... ☐ ☐

2 Good lighting .... ☐ ☐

3 A computer .... ☐ ☐

4 A strong and reliable Wi-Fi signal .... ☐ ☐

5 Relevant software .... ☐ ☐

Good to have

1 A wireless ergonomic mouse .... ☐ ☐

2 Some noise-cancelling headphones .... ☐ ☐

3 A footrest .... ☐ ☐

4 A document holder .... ☐ ☐

5 A 1080-pixel webcam with a good microphone .... ☐ ☐

In focus

BAD WI-FI?
It's not uncommon to suffer Wi-Fi problems when working at home, especially if you're taking up lots of bandwidth with video calls and collaborative software. Short of upgrading your connection, there are things you can do. If your home is spread out, the walls are thick, or you're working on a different floor to your router, you may find the signal doesn't reach your office. Try installing a Wi-Fi range extender to boost coverage. However, this won't help if the problem lies with your provider. If you are experiencing issues, connecting your computer to the internet via your smartphone – known as "tethering" – can be a helpful back-up. Go to "Settings" and look for "Mobile Hotspot" if you're on Android or "Personal Hotspot" on an iPhone.

Using instant messaging

Faster than email, instant messaging allows you to chat in real time with colleagues. While it is great for talking through issues at a distance, it can also be highly distracting. Set your app's preferences to suit your needs.

Communicating in real time

Instant messaging has become a popular workplace tool, allowing people to talk more freely without worrying about having their comments recorded in a paper trail. Apps such as Slack and Microsoft Teams let colleagues connect and receive responses instantly, but such immediacy also requires new considerations regarding etiquette and expectations. Also be aware that your staff may use instant messaging for gossiping, wasting time in the process.

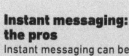

Instant messaging: the pros

Instant messaging can be **quicker than email**, not least because you can see if the person is available to answer your message before you send it. In some cases you'll even be notified when they read it. Instant-messaging apps let you set up **direct conversations** between two or three people, as well as establish "channels" that include your wider team or whole organization. You can even create **non-work themed channels** for general chat, social events, or trivia, which can help reinforce a sense of **unity in a dispersed team**.

Over 750,000 organizations around the world use **Slack**, with over 122,000 of them **paying for** its service

In focus

KEEPING INSTANT-MESSAGING TOOLS TIDY

Instant-messaging apps allow you to take a focused, real-time approach to collaborative working. But too many groups and too much chatter can quickly get out of control. Follow a few rules for keeping things organized:

- Label each instant-messaging channel or working group clearly to avoid confusion.
- Only create a new group when absolutely necessary, and archive discussions from completed projects.
- Only invite people who need to hear about the topic in hand.
- Encourage people to share links to live documents if helpful, but you should also maintain a proper cloud-based filing system.
- Check in with individuals to make sure your instant-messaging tools are supporting, rather than hindering, collaboration.
- For complicated issues, take the discussion off chat and schedule a proper meeting.

Instant messaging: the cons

The immediacy of instant messaging can be one of its big problems. Receiving a request when you are visibly online can put the **pressure on to respond** straight away, distracting you from more important tasks. Instant messaging can also be "noisy" with **frequent notifications**, particularly if you subscribe to lots of channels. This can be worse if you have the app installed on your phone, making it **harder to set boundaries** between work and home life. It's important to make the software work for you: set your status to "away" when you're unavailable and edit the app's preferences to limit notifications.

Choosing video-conferencing tools

Video conferencing is a vital component of remote managing. It allows dispersed colleagues to connect face to face, encouraging a sense of unity that audio conferencing alone cannot achieve. There are many apps out there, so be sure to compare the options to discover which suits you best.

To pay or not to pay?

Video conferencing isn't just about seeing your staff and colleagues' faces. You can also share what's on your screen, record meetings, exchange files, and make audio-only calls. Many apps also include an instant-messaging function, which is useful for sharing links to documents and asking questions without interrupting whoever's speaking.

As a manager, it's important to look at your own and your staff's requirements, both now and in the future, in order to understand what features you need before you decide which one of the many available apps is best for you. Popular services include Zoom, Slack, Microsoft Teams, Webex, Google Meet, and GoToMeeting. In most cases these offer a free version with limited features, but if you want to unlock more options, such as longer meeting times or the ability to add more participants, you will need to upgrade to a paid-for package. Make sure you compare different apps and different plans to avoid paying for add-ons you don't need, or missing out on those you do.

Number of participants

Zoom's free package allows **up to 100 participants** per meeting, and other apps have similar limits. For all but the biggest teams that should be **more than enough**, but think about what you need the app for. If, say, you want to host all-staff meetings, you may need to upgrade.

Meeting time

None of the apps mentioned here offer meetings lasting **longer than an hour** with their free packages. But it's worth considering **how long your conferences really need to be**. Shorter meetings will give time back to you and your staff to get work done.

Screen sharing

Rather than trying to describe something, **you can show it** by sharing your screen. This is normally a free feature, but you may need a paid-for package to allow **more than one person** to use it at a time. Will that suit your needs? Or do you want all staff to be able to share their screens?

Recording

The ability to record meetings is helpful **when people can't attend them**, or you are presenting a lot of information that warrants a closer look. It is also useful when you want to play back **job interviews or user research** conducted via video to others in your organization.

Software integration

You may prefer to use a video app that **integrates with the software suite** you already use for more seamless working. Microsoft Teams is designed to slot into Microsoft 365, while Google Meet and LogMeIn's GoToMeeting also fit into their makers' **wider product range**.

Usability

Video conferencing is meant to make life easier for remote employees. Be sure to **test the user experience of different apps on different devices**, keeping in mind that some of your employees may be accessing meetings from **smartphones or tablets**.

Collaborating on and sharing documents

Today's online file-sharing platforms that store data in the "cloud" provide useful tools for remote managers and their staff. But as well as allowing you to easily exchange, access, and edit information, they also carry an increased data protection risk.

Keeping track of collaboration

Real-time digital collaboration tools offer many benefits for remote managers. Online file-sharing platforms allow you and your staff to share documents, track changes, manage different versions of them, and tag other users wherever they are. They are also important in giving you a "single source of truth" to refer to. With your staff working in their own spaces, misunderstandings and duplication of work become greater dangers. Being able to see the latest versions of documents in one place means you can quickly view how far a task has progressed without having to chase multiple employees for their input.

> **Tip**
>
> **CHECK TWICE, ACT ONCE**
> Collaborating remotely means making sure **all parties** know what's required. If a request isn't clear, don't fill in the gaps yourself. **Ask before you act.**

Training the team

Data protection is a **serious legal business obligation**. Your staff must understand how cyberattacks and data leaks happen, and how to prevent them (see pp.44–45). While it can be tempting to attach a file to an email, or send it to a personal account, it could **end up in the wrong hands** – with legal consequences for both you and your organization.

Getting to know the cloud

Cloud computing, the delivery of tools and services over the internet, is the basis of online file-sharing suites such as Microsoft 365 and Google Drive. Rather than being stored on a computer hard drive or company server, they host your information in remote data centres where you can access it at any time, from anywhere. Microsoft 365 features browser-based versions of programs, such as Word, PowerPoint, and Excel, while Google Drive is part of Google's larger suite of tools. Useful standalone tools include whiteboard apps, such as Miro, which help re-create the experience of brainstorming in a room together, and project management services such as Jira, Trello, and Monday.com.

Setting permissions

One benefit of online document collaboration is that it lets you set permissions to **determine who can access a file and how much they can change**. Use these tools carefully: they normally range from giving one person read-only access to making a document editable by anyone. You must keep a tight rein on sensitive data.

Rolling back the clock

One key benefit of online document collaboration is that it helps establish version control. **This is important if two or more people are working on the same document** at different times, letting them see what's changed and then mark their own changes. If something goes wrong, **document-sharing platforms let you "roll back"** to a previous version, it's easy to undo the mess.

Deciding how to communicate

You need to remain in frequent contact with colleagues when managing at a distance, whether via phone call, email, instant messaging, or face-to-face video chat. Each of these methods is great in certain situations, but less so in others, so how do you choose which one is best?

Picking the best method

Before you choose a communication method, think about how you would like to receive the message you're about to convey. If it's not something you'd be happy learning on a group instant-messaging channel, or it doesn't need a meeting to solve, factor that in. Staff members will thank you for not adding unnecessary calls or lengthy emails to their day, as well as for not having serious or private matters pop up in a chat window.

> **Tip**
>
> **CURB THE CAPITALS**
> Avoid writing messages in **capital letters** – it can look like you're shouting. Also be sparing in your use of **question and exclamation marks**: too many can be annoying and confusing.

Video call
As a remote manager, you may feel the urge to talk to your staff face to face more often, but be sparing with video calls to avoid wasting people's time. Is a meeting necessary? Whose presence is essential?

Telephone
Phone calls are good for providing emotional support, and for getting a quick yes or no. But be aware they can be intrusive, and you may catch the person when they can't access the info you need.

Case study

NOT HOW YOU MEANT IT?
Written communications are open to misinterpretation, and sarcasm can be particularly difficult to convey. In 2010, US firm Sarcasm, Inc went so far as to trademark a new form of punctuation, the "SarcMark", to flag up when a phrase was intended sarcastically. The solution met with mixed reviews, but it served to highlight the lengths sometimes needed to make your meaning clear. While sarcasm is usually best avoided in the workplace, it's important to consider how any message you write might be understood. It can help to read your email aloud after writing it, or even better, if it's not urgent, to step away from it for a while, then return to review it with fresh eyes.

Email
Emails are the best way to relay a lot of information, but structure them carefully to avoid misinterpretation (see pp.50–51). They are also useful as you can refer back to them, and let you prove information was given.

Instant messaging
When you need a document or link in a hurry, a chat app is often the way to go. Just be aware that the quick response you want may not be possible, and that messaging does not suit more formal issues.

Using time-management tools

Working remotely can make time management more of a challenge. Without the structure of commuting and being in the workplace, you can find your days getting away from you as distractions and disruptions mount. Use a time-management tool to keep you and your staff on track.

Tracking progress

Nobody wants to feel they are being monitored, but as a manager, you do need to be able to see what your employees are working on at a glance. Time-management apps provide you with a reliable way to organize your own and your staff's time, monitor progress, identify efficiencies, and meet deadlines when working remotely. All of the services listed here offer an initial free trial, but you will need to subscribe to get the full package.

In focus

FRAGMENTING TIME

Working remotely means you are more likely to experience "fragmented time" – when spiralling meeting requests break up your schedule, leaving you with fewer hours to get work done. Keeping your shared time-management platform up to date lets you or other employees see the status of a task without having to chase for an update. When your time is limited, it's important to make the most of it.

RescueTime

This is available for individuals or teams, and **tracks your computer activity** to generate daily or weekly **scores that measure productivity**. It also lets you block distracting sites.

Toggl Track

This time-tracking app is designed to manage projects across teams, giving you a clear picture of your **work habits and completed tasks**. It offers insights into productivity, and helps you to spot and reduce **"scope creep"** – when a project's requirements and goals change from those agreed.

WorkflowMax

A suite of tools for managing projects remotely, from offering quotes, to tracking time, and managing staff. It's also useful for freelancers, because it allows you to **track your billable time** while you work, entering hours per client, and submitting timesheets.

Time Doctor

Sitting at the more forensic end of time management, this **monitors your team's computer use** – including mouse and keyboard activity, and time spent on websites and applications – and **sends reports to managers and staff**. While it's useful for highlighting lost productivity, be aware that this kind of tracking may not be well received.

Protecting data

From sending unencrypted files to losing laptops, lapses in cyber-security are all too easy when working outside of the workplace. The cost of a data breach can run into the millions, not to mention the damage to your organization's reputation, so maintaining strict measures is vital.

Backing up your data

Keep important data safe by creating regular backups. In a smaller operation you can do this manually, but this is time consuming. If you use a cloud service to store your data offsite, it will provide regular backups, but ensure you also understand the security measures your provider offers. These include:

Encryption: Unencrypted data can be leaked, sold, or used against you.
Firewalls: Cloud firewalls create a security barrier to block distributed denial of service (DDoS) attacks, which aim to take down your site by overrunning it with internet traffic.
Identity and access management (IAM): This attaches permissions to each user's identity to track who they are and what they're allowed to do.
Failover plans: These detail how your provider will enable your organization to carry on in the event of a problem at its end.

53%

of **companies** have over 1,000 sensitive files that every employee can access

In focus

UNDERSTANDING THE THREATS

Cyber-security is about protecting yourself from two key threats: cyber-crime and in-house lapses. The first involves a third party attacking your organization. It might hold sensitive data to ransom, launch a DDoS attack to take down your website, or intercept communications and steal login credentials. In-house lapses – leaving a laptop in a taxi, for example – cause sensitive information to fall into the wrong hands, or the public sphere. Both kinds of data breach can be embarrassing, expensive, and even lead to legal action. Pick the right cloud-storage providers and educate your employees to protect your organization as comprehensively as you can.

Educating employees

Limit potential for data breaches by ensuring staff stick to agreed cyber-security measures. If your organization provides employees with IT equipment, it will have control over those devices, and should have cyber-security policies in place – it's essential to keep these up to date. If it doesn't, adhering to security policies is even more important. Using personal email accounts or USB drives is tempting, but it moves data outside of your security loop. If data is hacked or lost, the cost will impact the organization.

Using devices in public places

Be aware that remote staff members may be working in cafés or shared work spaces, where they might be accessing data over unsecured Wi-Fi or exposing it to the eyes of people outside of the company. Ensure staff install a virtual private network (VPN) on their machines. This allows them to use public Wi-Fi safely, creating an encrypted "tunnel" for their data that makes it hard to unscramble or intercept. While there are free VPN providers, it's worth paying for a premium service, such as NordVPN, PrivateVPN, or SurfShark.

Tip

SHARE RESPONSIBILITY
It's good to have a resident cyber-security expert within your business, but **don't leave the responsibility to just one person**. For businesses operating remotely, it's important that **everyone understands** agreed practices and secure ways of working.

Remote working with Agile

Designed for software developers but now found in many businesses, the Agile process of working is a useful way of making longer-term goals more manageable by breaking them down into shorter chunks. You can easily adapt it to a remote setup using a few tech tools.

Using Agile at a distance

The Agile process is about incremental progress: you break down big objectives into smaller parts, known as "sprints", in order to move forward more efficiently. Sprints often last two weeks or so, and include a small number of agreed goals. After each sprint is complete, you and your staff review what went well and what needs more attention to help inform how to approach the next sprint.

Agile working requires daily catch-up meetings with the whole team to continually monitor progress. These meetings can easily be replicated from a distance using video-conferencing apps such as Zoom, Slack, and Microsoft Teams (see pp.36-37).

Planning as a group

Agile working uses planning sessions in which staff members **place sticky notes on a whiteboard**, often under headings such as "Do more of", "Do less of", and "Do better". You can replicate the experience of gathering in a room together using **virtual whiteboard apps** such as Miro, which allows staff to add notes and agree with comments from others. Other virtual whiteboard tools include Bluescape, InVision, JamBoard, and Lucidchart.

While each **Agile task** only lasts a couple of weeks, you must also keep **a clear view of your longer-term goals**

Monitoring progress

Agile emphasizes monitoring **the progress of each task step by step** – from the moment you ask an employee to tackle a specific job through to its completion. Even employees sharing the same physical space use **project management platforms such as Jira** to provide clear visual representations of progress. Jira lets you assign tasks to staff members, who can then update you on their progress and any problems they encounter. It also lets you create a backlog for things that don't fit in a sprint just yet. Alternatives include **Monday.com, Asana, Trello, and Basecamp**.

Seeing the bigger picture

While each Agile sprint only lasts a couple of weeks, you must also keep a clear view of your longer-term goals. A **Gantt chart** can help here – it's a way of visualizing a work schedule using blocks of colour set across a date range, making it easier to understand **what's coming up, and the resources you'll need**. Many project management tools that work well with Agile also have a Gantt chart function, including Asana, Workzone, Microsoft Project, and ProofHub.

Mastering
remote
communication

When collaborating from a distance, communicating well becomes even more important. To be a successful remote manager, take extra care to follow good etiquette, use the best medium for your message, and make everyone feel included and valued, whatever their position, time zone, or level of expertise.

Writing effective emails

When you are working away from your colleagues and staff, it's even more important to make sure your emails are clear and polite. Send messages that are easily understood and include the necessary information to get the responses you require.

Using email

Emails are useful for certain types of task: for example, asking a colleague to complete a piece of work, sending a project update, getting an opinion on something, or congratulating the whole team on a job well done. If you want a response to your email, say so. If the matter is important, provide a deadline instead of assuming your email will be seen and dealt with as quickly as you expect. For complicated or emotional topics, it's better to choose a phone call or private chat window.

Show respect
Start with a greeting and sign off with a thank you. Address recipients by name, unless you're sending to a large group. **Say please** when you ask someone to do something. **Say thanks** when it's done.

Be clear
Use simple language, free of jargon if possible. **Avoid overly specialized terms** unless addressing technical staff. Get to the point quickly, convey the necessary information, or state what it is you require.

Make it accessible
Choose a legible font type and size, using the **bold font style** to highlight key sections and bullet points to **make information easier to read** and absorb.

Getting the tone right

When writing emails address everyone, whether they're an external client or a staff member, with the same level of respect. People can't gauge your tone in written text as well as they can in speech, so make an effort to be professional and polite. Read over each email before you send it – how would you feel about receiving it? If you do not yet have any team or company guidelines for writing emails, consider implementing some to cover both in-house and external communications.

Tip

AVOID EMAIL EMBARRASSMENT

Write your message and **check it over before you add the email addresses** you want to send it to. This stops you sending **half-finished emails** by accident.

Write a clear subject line

Write your subject line *after* you've written your email. **Use it to tell the person what your email is about** and whether you expect an answer. For example: "New client request – can you help?"

Include contact details

Add your name, job title, phone number, and any other work contact details to the end of your emails. You can do this automatically **by adding a signature** to your email account.

Consider your recipients

Does everyone you are sending it to need to read it? If not, take them off the recipient list. Bothering people with **irrelevant emails** could cause them to skip over the message you really do need a response to.

Mastering phone calls and messages

A voice call at the right moment is sometimes the most effective way to deliver and receive the information you need. Learning how to hold positive phone conversations and leave clear messages helps you save time, maintain good working relationships, and get the best out of your staff.

Knowing when to pick up the phone

In a world that relies increasingly on email and chat software, a traditional phone call can help you find quick solutions to problems. In general, use the phone to: clarify a point; defuse a situation where a colleague is unhappy; or to provide emotional support. If you're calling someone who works remotely, note that yours might be the only voice they hear that day. Make an effort to connect, ask how they are, and, above all, listen. Not everyone likes communicating by phone, though, so try to find out what's best for each individual.

> **Tip**
>
> **REDUCE BACKGROUND NOISE**
> Make a call on your own from **a quiet room**. If you're at home, reduce interruptions and noise by telling other people in your household not to disturb you. **Avoid eating or drinking** during the call.

Leaving the perfect message

Whether you're leaving a message for a stranger or an acquaintance, say hello, state your name clearly, and say why you're calling. Tell them when you can be contacted, especially if you work flexible hours and days, and say if you need a reply urgently. If the person doesn't have your phone number, recite it slowly once, then repeat it. Keep your message to a maximum of 30 seconds long, if possible. Give them time to receive the message, get the information you've asked for, and find a convenient time to call you back.

Check your timing

Think before you dial: is the other person working right now? **Bear in mind any flexible working arrangements** or time-zone differences. If the person you want to speak to is on leave, send an email instead. Or even better, wait until they return to work.

Be polite

It doesn't matter if you're under pressure or in a hurry, you still have to **be pleasant, polite, and professional** on the phone. Remember to ask how the other person is. If the person needs some extra support, lend a sympathetic ear, and offer to help.

Speak clearly

Never assume the person you're calling can hear you perfectly – the line may be poor or they may be in a noisy location. Speak clearly and **not too quickly**, especially when leaving a message or voicemail in a rush. Watch out for the volume of your voice – **not too loud**, not too soft.

Listen actively

Concentrate on what the other person is saying and **don't interrupt** them mid-sentence. Take notes if you need to and ask questions after they've finished speaking. It can help to **repeat points back** to make sure you've understood them fully.

Respect other preferences

Don't be offended if you don't get a call back after leaving your voicemail. It might be **more convenient** for the other person to send you a quick email with their answer.

Respecting the calendar

Your online calendar is essential for organizing your own time, and that of others. It helps you keep track of deadlines and meetings, and shows when you are available. Be sure to share it and keep it up to date.

Making your work life visible

Whatever online calendar app you have (Outlook, Google Calendar, Asana), be sure to use it, and insist that your staff do the same. This will allow you to see what they are doing and when (something remote working can make difficult), helping you to plan workflows more effectively. Shared calendars are also useful for tackling staff time-management and discipline issues.

MON	TUE

Keeping your schedule current
Be a stickler about updating your calendar. This is helpful for colleagues who use your schedule for planning. Try to **reserve some space free each day for supporting your staff**. That way you show you are an approachable manager, rather than one tangled up in senior meetings.

Booking leave
There might be a separate company system for booking leave, but **add everything to your own calendar, too**. Label days off as all-day events and get your staff to do the same, or create a separate **staff holiday calendar**. The latter has the benefit of clearly showing who's away week to week.

Never assume your meeting is more important than another entry on someone's calendar. If it's urgent, **politely ask** the person concerned if it's possible to use that time slot

Sharing your calendar

Usually, your calendar lets anyone in your organization see your blocked time slots and request meetings. Most online calendars let you set permission levels to share fuller details with designated people – allowing them to see "all details", for example – but there's no need to share entire schedules with the whole firm.

WED	THU	FRI

Blocking out non-negotiables
Always eating in front of your computer?
Block out a proper lunch break in your calendar and suggest others do the same. Do you have a recurring appointment like a school run or yoga class you can't miss? Mark it on your schedule – it will **discourage others from trying to overbook your time**.

Choosing a time
If you want to book a larger meeting with lots of attendees, **find out if anything else significant is happening around the same time**. Consider other company events, upcoming national holidays, or religious celebrations that may impact your planning.

Encouraging productivity
Help others prepare for your meeting by **adding useful information to the calendar entry**. Agenda points, supporting documents, links to relevant content, questions you need answers to – anything that will help you achieve your aim. Note: **if your meeting slot spans more than 90 minutes, it's probably too long**. Can you break it into two?

Moderating meetings

It's the moderator's job to oversee and facilitate a meeting. In a virtual environment, this requires having a solid plan tailored to what you aim to achieve, a good understanding of the technology, and an inclusive and respectful approach that leaves no one out.

Meeting virtually

You can meet via group phone calls, video calls, or via hybrid meetings, where some people are there in person and others join by phone or video link. For training or conference-style sessions, consider switching your usual video app for a specific webinar tool (see pp.86–87), which are well suited to presentations led by one or more speakers. Whatever your format, be sure to distribute an agenda beforehand, along with any relevant information your attendees might benefit from seeing before the discussion starts. Helping everyone to arrive prepared saves time on lengthy explanations, meaning you can get to the point quickly (and finish on time).

Case study

A DAY OFF FROM MEETINGS

Meetings can take up a lot of your working day when you're a manager, leaving you with little time to do other things. As part of its response to the Covid-19 pandemic in 2020, Amsterdam-based cloud technology firm Container Solutions introduced a "no-meeting Wednesday" to help its busy team. It proved so popular that the company decided to make it a permanent rule.

Do your planning

Ask yourself **what you want to achieve** in your meeting. Who needs to be there to make it happen? What time of day would work for those colleagues? How long does the meeting need to be? If you want to encourage lots of **live discussion**, choose a smaller group. Decide any tasks you need to delegate, such as taking notes, running the technical side, or keeping track of your agenda and timings.

Understand your tech

Make sure you're comfortable using the meeting technology. **Go over the basic features** with less experienced staff if they need it. It's better to have **participants on equal terms** (such as everyone having their cameras on during a video call), but make exceptions if a colleague has a poor internet connection or is anxious about appearing on video.

Explain the terms

Be clear about **how participants should behave**. For example, request that attendees save questions to the end and don't talk over each other. Ask people to **mute their microphones** when they're not speaking, especially if they're typing. You might prefer to collect comments and questions via your tool's chat feature or in a shared live document.

Include everyone

Introduce any new staff members or guest speakers and use people's names when you address them. On video calls, use your own facial expressions and voice to **engage others and encourage participation**. Watch faces to check for signs that someone would like to speak. Or if you can't see them, ask if anyone has anything else to say and **listen carefully** when they do. You can also invite people to send you their ideas after the meeting.

Following group chat etiquette

Instant messaging is useful for solving problems in real time as a team, letting you ask questions and give answers quickly without interrupting the rhythm of your day. But while the medium is less formal, remain respectful and use it wisely.

Guiding your staff

Encourage employees to be professional and respectful during any work instant-messaging chats. As a manager, lead by example – try to keep conversations on topic: in the #ProjectY channel, only discuss Project Y. To avoid overwhelming others in group chats, you can switch to one-to-one private messages for detailed discussion that's better kept between two. Set up dedicated social channels to give staff a more relaxed forum for general discussion – this helps teams to bond and share experiences unrelated to work.

> **Tip**
>
> **CONSIDER YOUR AUDIENCE**
> Be mindful of colleagues who are not using their first language or are from **different cultures**. Make your language **clear and appropriate**, and **explain** any new abbreviations or less obvious terms.

In focus

THE FIVE GOLDEN RULES OF MESSAGING ETIQUETTE

1. Don't put others under undue pressure to reply immediately. Give people space – they may be busy, not know the answer immediately, or simply want a break.
2. Respect a colleague's decision to set their status to "away" or "busy". A message sent while someone is unavailable may go unanswered. The recipient may also feel that they are being overly pressured.
3. Think about whether someone needs to be involved in a conversation before you include them. People receive lots of messages every day. If they don't need to be in the chat, don't add them.
4. Remember that slang and casual language may not translate well or be appropriate for the situation.
5. Don't use instant messaging tools for important announcements. Updates that have far-reaching consequences require a more formal approach.

I set my status to "busy" but the messages keep coming

So many acronyms, I'm a bit lost

I think this conversation would work better on the phone

I wish we could just talk about the project in hand

Running video calls

When managing remotely, a video call might be the closest you get to meeting colleagues face to face. Use the opportunity to show your support for staff and their work, helping you unite as a team, and get things done. Follow a few key steps to make everything run smoothly.

Hosting a video meeting

According to business professor Gianpiero Petriglieri, too much virtual video contact without the benefit of physical human contact can make people feel "overwhelmed and deprived at once". So although video calls are useful, only book one when it suits the task. Stick to your agreed time frame by sending out a clear agenda and setting a time limit for each point. Set a positive mood and take on a facilitator role, speaking clearly and listening to all voices, not just the dominant ones. If you don't have an answer to a question, say you'll respond after the call and move on. Technical issues? Turning off cameras and continuing with just audio can help.

Managing participants

For calls with just a few participants, you can be less formal and encourage more of a live conversation. For larger groups, get people to submit questions and comments via the chat function, an online poll, or a shared live document (such as a Google Doc). This way everyone can add their thoughts without competing to be heard. Although you should, of course, look presentable and act professionally on every video call, take extra care when meeting via video with an external client or supplier. Unusual or overly casual dress can distract from the purpose of the meeting and have an impact on how your organization is viewed from the outside.

ASK YOURSELF...
Am I ready to host a video call?   **YES   NO**

1 Have I checked what's **visible in the background**? ☐ ☐

2 Have I **looked in the mirror** to check I'm presentable? ☐ ☐

3 Is my **internet connection strong** enough? ☐ ☐

4 Is my **microphone working**, and do I know how to turn it on and off? ☐ ☐

5 Have I **circulated the agenda**? ☐ ☐

6 Am I **prepared for the specific content** of this meeting? ☐ ☐

7 Have I asked others in my household **not to disturb me** for the duration? ☐ ☐

8 Have I checked that attendees are happy for me to **record the call**? ☐ ☐

9 If I'm not recording, have I asked someone **to take minutes**? ☐ ☐

In focus

"I THINK YOU'RE ON MUTE ..."

It's a familiar phrase for remote workers. Forgetting to turn your microphone on before you start speaking is easily done. If this happens to you or someone else on a video call, be professional and get the conversation back on track quickly. When you're not talking, mute the mic, reducing background noise for everyone.

Presenting virtually

Giving a presentation online requires you to overcome the technical challenges of video conferencing. But it also means adjusting your approach to the fact your audience is watching you on a screen. Use more visuals, clear body language, and lively speech to present effectively.

Presenting with confidence

Much of the advice on making video calls (see pp.60–61) applies just as much to giving successful virtual presentations. Check your camera and microphone, be sure to stick to timings, and set a positive mood. But there are also a few extra pointers that will help you present your topic clearly.

Know your subject

Run through your presentation aloud **at least twice** before delivering it. This helps you to speak more naturally and clearly, and **project confidence**. Reduce the amount of text you present, choosing images or video clips to **grab your audience's attention**.

Practise screen sharing

If it's your first time, **do a trial run** with a friend or colleague to make sure you know how to share documents on your screen with your audience. **Close unrelated files** and browser windows to ensure there's no chance of sharing confidential information.

Avoid interruptions

Turn off your email and chat notifications to **minimize distractions** and the risk of sharing private messages. If you're working at home, let family members or housemates know when you're due to present so they will **leave you in peace**.

Whether you're addressing three people or a hundred, do a **last-minute check** in the mirror before logging on

Press record

Consider recording your presentations to **distribute later** to those unable to attend, or for future new starters to watch. If the session is interactive, check your attendees are **happy to be recorded**.

DON'T PANIC

If you run into a **technical hitch** such as a frozen screen, poor picture, or broken sound don't panic. Ask for a moment to see if you can **troubleshoot the issue**. If you can't, apologize, and ask to re-schedule.

Engage your audience

Greet everyone at the start of the session and **thank them for joining**. If you're starting the call with your face on camera, **don't forget to smile**, sit up straight, and engage. It can help to slightly exaggerate your body language on camera, **be more animated** in your speech, and talk at a slightly slower pace than usual. It's a nice touch to finish your presentation by **saying goodbye "face to face"** at the end.

Gather input

For formal presentations, ask people to **save their questions until the end**. For informal ones, you can choose whether or not to welcome interruptions as you go. For very large groups, get people to **submit questions and comments via the chat function** or a live document, and deal with them at the end.

Hosting virtual events

Virtual events require as much planning as their real-world equivalents. As well as organizing speakers and invitations, you need to pick the right platform and stick to a tight schedule. But whether it's a conference or virtual away-day, the key is not to treat it like a larger work meeting.

Making a plan

With more people working remotely, online events are increasingly common, from small public lectures to larger conferences. With so much technology available, hosting one is now much more accessible to all types of professional. Identify the purpose of your event – is it social or will attendees be working? Calculate your running time, if it's more than a couple of hours, factor in breaks, activities, or other ways to keep people engaged. Break the event into sections, such as introduction, presentation and live poll, first guest speaker. Get all the details down in a plan, assemble helpers, and start delegating tasks, such as compiling the guest list or agenda.

Choosing your technology

Research a suitable platform that works for your specific event. Work out what you need: appearances by speakers, polls to gather live feedback, a virtual whiteboard, "breakout rooms" for group activities, and so on (see pp.36–37). When you've chosen your appropriate technology, test it with a colleague by running through the agenda in sequence.

Promoting your event

For an event that's open to external attendees, you need to provide more than just the date, time, and duration. Consider using a designer to create branded e-invitations. You may need to send these out more than once to get all the responses, and you should send reminders to make sure people attend.

Creating your content

Make sure any presentations are eye-catching and not too text heavy. Think about adding interactive elements, such as ice breakers, quizzes, and polls, or presenting some of your information in video format. If you're giving out prizes or providing props for activities, send these out to attendees well in advance. Book any guest speakers early, making sure they understand exactly what you need from them on the day. To ensure everything runs smoothly when running the event, put someone in charge of keeping everyone to time.

Collecting feedback

After the event, send out anonymous feedback forms to find out what participants thought, and what they would like to see another time. Use this information to make your next event even better.

90%

of virtual event organizers **send out surveys** to gather feedback from attendees

In focus

BRINGING IN THE PROFESSIONALS

For bigger occasions with lots of attendees, consider getting an external event management company involved. Event industry experts are used to reproducing the elements of an in-person event in a virtual environment. They take care of the planning, the technical side, and the smooth running of the proceedings. Work with them to create content and manage the event. Then you can sit back and relax when it comes to hosting the event.

Overcoming time zones

As a manager, you may have colleagues and staff working in different times zones from you. While this can present challenges, you can overcome these through careful time-management, clear communication, and effective planning.

Managing a global workforce

Flexible and remote working mean you can recruit from anywhere in the world. The result is a strong talent pool to draw on that will feed into the success of your business. The tricky part is managing people who don't work the same hours. Some overlap in shifts is best for live collaboration, but if you can't work at the same time, you can still work together efficiently with good planning. It's important to respect different schedules, cultures, and personalities, and make sure everyone feels like a valued contributor. Be sure to make work/life balance a priority for every staff member, wherever they are.

Clever time management

Make the most of periods when everyone is online – a quick weekly video meeting **creates a solid team dynamic**. Use "asynchronous collaboration" (teamwork that's not done at the same time) to cover the rest of the workload, **using agreed feedback times to avoid delays**. Use messaging apps or live documents to ask for input, so that answers are **waiting for you when you log in the next day**. Sometimes, you might need to join a meeting later or earlier than you'd like. When working across time zones, take turns to do this so the same people aren't always being asked to compromise their plans.

Tip

CHECK THE TIME
Do you need to send that message **immediately?** Use sites such as timeanddate.com to check the time where your recipient lives. See if your tools allow you to **schedule messages** to send later.

Clear communication

Speak and write in simple terms, especially to those working in a second language. Think about **compiling clear communication guidelines for your staff**. If you're recording a presentation to circulate later, speak clearly, and summarize what you've achieved at the end. When setting tasks, **give enough detail for them to be completed while you're logged off**. State a desired response time or a firm deadline using time-zone abbreviations: "11am GMT", not just "11am".

Detailed planning

Recording **all work shifts on a shared team calendar** highlights crossover points and shows who is available when. Ask someone in each location to **record significant dates** for their territory: national holidays, religious celebrations, and even key seasonal changes that could affect work, such as monsoon. Add working hours and time-zone abbreviations to staff email signatures to provide a regular reminder.

Leading from a **distance**

Managing a dispersed team doesn't change the underlying qualities of good leadership, but it does change the context in which you apply those qualities. As a remote manager, it's your role to lead and motivate your staff wherever they are located, and also to recruit and coordinate new members whom you may never meet in person.

04

Becoming a long-distance leader

As a remote leader, managing your employees and projects comes with extra challenges. How do you keep your team motivated or monitor their progress? Start by assessing the strengths and weaknesses of the situation, and address the issues accordingly.

Assessing how your organization works

There's no "one-size-fits-all" approach to remote working, so you must assess the people you work with and the logistics of leading them. You might be based in the office managing a team dispersed across the country, or across several countries. Alternatively, your team might work from a single site and you are the only remote element. Your organization could be "part-remote", where meeting in person is still possible, or "fully remote" in which all communication is from a distance.

You might also have staff working part-time or flexible hours, or in different time zones.

Understanding your team

Think about how your team works. If you use an "Agile" working model (see pp.46–47), you'll be familiar with quick-fire daily meetings. These are a good way for smaller teams dealing with rapid changes to keep track of progress, but they're not right for everyone. For example, if you manage

> ### Tip
>
> **POST PROGRESS**
> **Project-management tools** such as Jira and Trello can give you a high-level view of what's happening, but only if users **regularly update their progress**. Encourage your staff to post an update when they **complete a task** and to ensure any links to documents they include on the platform go to the latest versions of them.

In focus

HOW DO I KNOW THEY'RE WORKING?

When managing staff performing a specific task, it's common to track productivity, although is less appropriate for less processed-based roles. Dedicated software for tracking progress, such as a project-management platform, is essential, but using programs that monitor mouse clicks or keystrokes is understandably unpopular and probably a step too far. Remember that activity and achievement are not the same thing. By setting and agreeing measurable goals (see pp.12–13), you and your team members can agree on what's expected. Having honest conversations helps you to raise concerns and proactively address issues in ways that build trust.

a team of mobile sales representatives, you're unlikely to get everyone on the phone at the same time every day. While if you oversee a large factory-floor team with a well-established routine, a scheduled daily meeting will likely be more disruptive than helpful. You should tailor your approach to the practicalities of your employees' working day.

Understanding the Remote Leadership Model

The Remote Leadership Model is a simple way of visualizing the experience of leading from a distance. It uses three interlocking "gears" to show how your established leadership skills need to work with new technologies to drive your organization forward.

A wider view of leadership

Developed by management experts Kevin Eikenberry and Wayne Turmel, the Remote Leadership Model is a prompt to ask yourself key questions when leading remotely. It reminds you that when you manage from a distance, core leadership skills remain essentially the same, but what's happening around them changes. Remain open to new technologies and ways of working, and be willing and able to learn them – your skills as a leader don't operate in a vacuum. Use the model to help you zoom out and see how leading effectively involves interacting with changing practicalities, too.

The **job of leading** – what we do – hasn't changed nearly as much as **how we do it**

ASK YOURSELF...

Am I making the best use of my resources?

	YES	NO
1 What **tools do you have** to help you get the job done?	☐	☐
2 Are you **relying too much** on tools you're comfortable using and **avoiding new ones** that are better?	☐	☐
3 Have there been any times when you could have done a better job by **adopting new technology**?	☐	☐
4 Are there any tools, new or old, that **hinder your effectiveness**?	☐	☐
5 Are you taking the opportunity for **training in new technologies**?	☐	☐
6 Are you making sure **your staff have the opportunity for training**? (see pp.86–87)	☐	☐

Leadership and management

This is the largest gear, and represents you and the expectations placed upon you. This gear **is the same**, no matter where you're working. As a leader, the way you conduct yourself, the behaviours you exhibit, and the **responsibilities** that lie with you are the same as ever.

Tools and technology

This is the second-largest gear, which concerns **the resources you have at your disposal** to get the job done. If working remotely is something new to you and your staff, you may be faced with using technology that feels **unfamiliar and uncomfortable**. You can't rely on existing methods alone and must adapt.

Skill and impact

The third gear illustrates your success in bringing together the first two in order to lead your team from a distance. It's about selecting **the right tools at the right time**, but it will only function properly if you're **willing to adopt** new technology and learn how to use it.

Using the Three O Model of Leadership

The Three O Model provides a useful way of thinking about your role as a remote leader. By highlighting the interdependencies between "Outcomes", "Others", and "Ourselves", it illustrates the tricky balance you must maintain between directing and encouraging your staff.

Striving for balance

Your role as a leader is something of a balancing act. On the one hand, you need to inspire and encourage others towards achieving outcomes together; on the other, you need to fulfil the expected role of leader, being visible, and in control. This means you sit both within and at the head of the team – you can't achieve outcomes without them, but they can't flourish without your direction. As a remote leader, the challenge is to "lead from behind", which means staying visible and approachable, while giving others the space to fulfil their potential. By highlighting how the various factors involved – "Outcomes", "Others", and "Ourselves" – interlink, the Three O Model can help you decide the right balance to get the best out of your team.

Outcomes
As a leader, it's your job to pursue outcomes

Others
You can't achieve those outcomes without others

Ourselves
Others can't function at their best without you

Leadership doesn't revolve around you; rather, you bring who you are and how you lead to bear on **creating better outcomes** for others

Tip

GIVE PEOPLE CONTEXT
When people work remotely, employees may focus on their own goals and **lose sight** of the group's overall objectives. Use meetings to remind them how their goals **fit with the organization's wider purpose**.

Ensuring the right outcomes
Outcomes are **specific, tangible results** that you and your team are striving for. Without clear targets they can drift, especially when you're working apart, so it's more important than ever to **agree and set goals at an organizational, team, and individual level**. When expectations are clear, the outcomes you need are more likely to be achieved.

Working with others
You can't do everything yourself. Your success as a leader will depend on **your ability to get the best from others**. Working remotely means communication becomes more important than ever: to **build trust**, to give a sense of **shared purpose**, and to make sure everyone **feels comfortable** speaking up about what is and isn't working.

Keeping yourself in the equation
Accepting you are not the focus of everything isn't the same as removing yourself from the equation. The Three O Model explains that while you may not be the centre, you're still very much at the core. It's key to communicate **your vision and values**, so while it's good to get input, be clear about your expectations. When a decision sits with you, **be seen to make the call**.

Working with distributed teams

Thanks to modern technology, building and managing remote teams that operate from multiple locations is now a reality. But it is important to be aware of the underlying challenges that tech alone won't solve.

Maintaining a one-team approach

Team members based in a single location find it easy to interact, build trust, and reach a shared understanding of goals, behaviours, and ways of working, even if they come from different backgrounds. But this is harder for team members working remotely – particularly when some are based far more remotely than most. For example, if four members of a team are based in the UK, while one is in Germany, the latter could easily feel more isolated, affecting his or her engagement, and causing resentment. Make sure everyone, regardless of their location, feels that they're on an equal footing when it comes to voicing their opinions and contributing their own experiences. Ensure all team members are invited to everything – social activities as well as work-related engagements. You could also ask people to give a short, informal "day-in-the-life" presentation to give their colleagues an idea of how the team's work looks from their perspective.

60%
of **remote workers** feel they miss out on **important information** because it's communicated **in person**

Working with second-language speakers

If your team includes people working in a second language, be careful that meetings do not become dominated by native speakers, particularly those with strong personalities. People will feel frustrated if they can't get a word in, while others may be reticent to speak up, meaning good ideas don't get expressed. Limit the time taken up by vociferous team members and encourage quieter ones to contribute.

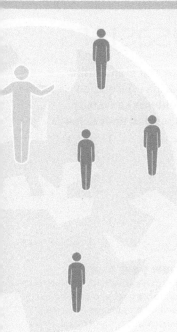

In focus

BUILDING A ROBUST KNOWLEDGE MANAGEMENT SYSTEM

Working across different locations brings practical challenges such as:

- How to deal with holidays observed in some countries but not others?
- How to operate across time zones so people can work together on tasks at the same time rather than through live collaboration?

Even with regular catch-ups, geography gets in the way. But setting up a knowledge management system that records, summarizes, and shares information allows all members of the team to access the data they need. It also helps everyone avoid missing out on important details that were communicated in person. One helpful approach is to use a central document management platform, such as Sharepoint, alongside a collaboration platform, such as Confluence. Confluence lets team members set up pages that summarize a project, including links to relevant resources stored on Sharepoint. These might include recorded meetings or summaries of key findings.

Tip

ASK BEFORE YOU RECORD

If you want to **record a video meeting** so others can watch it later, make sure everyone on the call knows and feels comfortable with that. Video apps normally display an onscreen banner to show when recording is in progress, but it's still **good practice to ask permission** (see p.63).

Planning for IT disasters

Being a remote manager means changing how you plan for the unexpected. Because work now relies on sharing information digitally and keeping it secure, serious IT problems can easily become a disaster. Take steps to prevent issues and limit damage.

Identify the threats
Working remotely means storing data offsite. This could leave you open to a ransomware attack with hackers encrypting your files and demanding money, or a denial-of-service attack (DDoS) crashing your website. Many providers now offer disaster recovery as a service (DRaaS), which not only stores your data but also protects it and builds in contingency planning.

Know your staff
An organization with a remote workforce needs to be able to reach its employees wherever they are. Your plan should contain up-to-date contact information, including email addresses, phone numbers, and emergency contacts. It should also designate team members' responsibilities in the event of a crisis and be stored in a number of secure locations.

Get a team in place
Disaster planning needs good communication. Put in place a dedicated team who can assess the potential impact of a disaster, as well as decide, document, and pass on key decisions to the rest of the organization. Think of them as first aiders for the business.

In focus

BUSINESS CONTINUITY vs DISASTER RECOVERY

These terms are often used interchangeably but are not the same. A business continuity plan is concerned with how the business keeps going in a crisis (fire, flood, outage...), describing how to keep disruption to a minimum and resume normal service. A disaster recovery plan is of more relevance in a remote situation, and concerns getting IT systems back online. It sets out how to re-establish access to data, power, software, hardware, and connectivity, as well as how to contact staff, customers, and shareholders.

Tip

DON'T FORGET HUMAN ERROR

Be aware that your own staff can put your data at risk. A recent survey of US remote workers found that **36 per cent had accessed work applications on a non-work device** and 45 per cent had shared a work computer with a spouse or a child. Make sure you have **clear remote-working rules** in place and share best practices across your organization.

Review it

An out-of-date plan is no use to anyone. Things change – personnel, processes, and new regulations could impact your procedures, especially if you work with sensitive data. Regularly review your plan to make sure it's fit for purpose.

Test it

You need to know you can reach your team and that they understand what's expected of them in a crisis. For example, set up "call trees" to give team members the responsibility to phone and notify others when they receive a call. These should be tested regularly to make sure they work.

Interviewing remotely

If you're hiring people remotely, be aware that the interview process will differ. You'll still be having a one-to-one conversation, but in a virtual environment, where you won't be able to spot the non-verbal cues that give valuable insight into an individual's character.

Upping your attention

Many aspects of interviewing remotely are the same as doing it in-person: you need to plan the meeting, ensure the candidate knows what's required, and find a suitable space. Ensure the tech you use works on the day, and have a contingency plan prepared. Be sure to communicate clearly to avoid any misunderstandings.

86%

of organizations are incorporating **new virtual technology** to interview **candidates**

1. Communicate the date and time clearly
Ensure the candidate receives the **invitation** and that the date and time are **convenient** for them.

2. Set expectations
Make sure the candidate **understands** the type of interview, the technology they'll need, and **how long** it's likely to take.

3. Prepare
For a professional interview, **test everything** – your camera, microphone, and Wi-Fi – and make sure you have a charger to hand.

5. Limit distractions
Find somewhere that's **quiet and private** for the duration of the interview. Tell colleagues and family members you'll be occupied for that length of time.

4. Have a back-up plan
This could be as simple as switching to a **phone interview**. If something goes wrong, take control of the situation and initiate your contingency plan, even if that means rescheduling.

6. Look professional
Dress as if you were conducting an in-person interview and try to find a **neutral, professional location**. If you can't, many video-call platforms offer virtual office backgrounds.

7. Watch and listen
Pay extra attention to **body language**, tone of voice, and engagement. It can be easy to forget that it's a live interview when you're watching a screen.

8. Give them space
Keep your **microphone on mute** when you're not speaking and leave a second or two before responding. Video calls can sometimes **suffer a lag** and talking over one another is frustrating.

Welcoming new starters remotely

Starting a new job can be awkward and nerve-racking for many people. Doing so remotely can be 10 times worse. As a manager, you should welcome new staff to your team with even more care than you would in a shared work space.

Setting the tone for day one

Make their first day a positive experience. Remember that remote starters don't get the chance to bump into co-workers around the building and they don't get taken out to lunch to get to know the team. But you can still provide a warm welcome, set expectations for the new role, and start each new staff member off on the right path.

Introduce key people

Start establishing a network by **introducing new staff to the rest of the team** and other important contacts. Invite all new starters to **join informal chat channels** and upcoming social events.

Get the tech side ready

It can take a while to grant **access to files and internal communication channels**. This can leave new starters, especially remote ones, **feeling cut off**. Do all you can to get the technical side of things sorted by the time they start.

Make a connection

Send out any new starter info in advance, plus a plan for what week one will look like. Also make sure any necessary training is set up. Book a **one-to-one welcome meeting** early on day one, preferably by video – smile, sit up, look at the person, and listen.

Explain company terms
When people start a new role remotely, they don't always come forward to ask about **unfamiliar terms**. Explain any organization-specific acronyms, jargon, and names of company tools. Include a company **glossary** to a new starter pack to explain key terms.

Get feedback
Ask the new recruit to provide feedback on the company's **induction procedures** to get a sense of what it's like to join your organization. Use the responses to **make the process better** for the next new employee.

Encourage questions
Tell new starters to ask as many questions as they like. You might need to respond to lots of chat messages or emails at first, but **put yourself in that person's shoes** and remember to be patient.

Be available
Book a regular **one-to-one catch-up** to check how the new person is getting on and **identify any issues**. You can offer additional support yourself or allocate a "buddy" – choose an experienced and personable staff member to do this.

Transitioning your staff to remote working

Migrating a team to remote working for the first time requires openness and collaboration. Seek your colleagues' and employees' thoughts, agree ground rules, and address their concerns to make the process as pain-free as possible.

Talking to your team

Start by speaking with your staff. Nobody knows how to do their jobs better than they do. Ask how they feel about the move, listen to their concerns, and find out what tools and technology they'll need. Agree your "rules of engagement": how you will stay in touch, how often, and which methods you will use. This will help to give your working days a defined structure and establish boundaries, which is particularly important if you are working from home. Your staff must feel able to take breaks and understand that working remotely doesn't mean being on call around the clock.

Trust

Your staff members will look to you, so **they need to know you're on board** with the changes as well.

Talk

Do it early and do it often. **The more notice** your staff has about the transition, **the better they'll feel**.

74%

of leaders believe they **involve employees** when managing change, but only **42%** of employees feel included

Continuing the conversation

As with any other major management change, keep your staff updated and check in with them to ask how things are going. Be aware that employees struggling with either the practical or emotional changes of remote working might not feel comfortable initiating the conversation. Set up regular check-ins as safe spaces in which people can tell you how they feel.

Agile working (see pp.46–47) often uses the concept of "fail fast". This is sometimes misunderstood, but the emphasis is on the second word.

CONTAGIOUS LEADERS

Organizations are increasingly recognizing the importance of emotional intelligence in leaders. The effect that managers' moods can have on those around them is significant. This is known as "emotional contagion", and a 2005 research paper found that it plays an important role in leadership. Your employees will take their emotional cues from you, so while you need to show empathy and understanding, you need to display confidence, too.

It means identifying and eliminating problems as early as possible, allowing the team to learn quickly and move on. Before you can deal with any teething issues, you need to know about them first, so liaise with staff regularly.

Time

Some members will adjust to the new setup quicker than others, so **be open and patient**.

Tools

Establish the essential tools and **put them in place** before any transition begins.

Training remotely

Staff expect their employers to invest in their development. That applies just as much for those working remotely as for those sharing a work space. As a remote manager, ensure your team has access to online materials to grow their skills from a distance.

Investing in the future

A well-designed staff-training programme not only helps your organization improve its collective skill set, but also motivates staff to stay longer and make more meaningful contributions to the business. In the absence of face-to-face learning, it's vital to have an engaging training and development programme available for employees, wherever they are.

In focus

TRY TEAM-LED TRAINING
Providing a suite of training materials that you as a manager think is useful is a good start. But also ask your staff what kind of professional training they would benefit from. Some of the best ideas come from employees who know how they want their careers to progress and have identified learning opportunities that you may not have thought of. Give employees the training they want – they will get much more out of it and be more likely to stay with the organization for longer.

Online courses
You can **make your own** company courses, **pay a third party** to provide them for you, or use training content from **an online provider**, such as LinkedIn Learning or Coursera.

Webinars
A webinar is an **online session** for a remote audience. It usually features a **presentation, a main speaker, and interaction** from attendees. Record your webinars to **keep as resources in your training library** for others to use.

Videos and podcasts

A compelling video grabs people's attention – make sure any audiovisual content you use has **high-quality pictures, sound, and subtitles**. Podcasts, pre-recorded audio files that are usually presented in a series, are easy to prepare in advance, and are popular with trainees.

Employee knowledge

Turn your staff's expertise into training materials. A blog post from one of your web developers or a how-to video by a call-centre worker can **help others pick up new skills** and learn about other parts of your organization.

Ask for feedback

Learn from trainees. Send out **anonymous surveys** to every attendee to gather honest feedback on how their training went.

One-to-one coaching

Ask people who are **experts in their areas of the business** to run virtual one-to-one coaching sessions with new starters, junior team members, or anyone who needs **training in highly technical subjects**.

94%

of employees say they would **stay longer** at a company that invested in their **learning and development**

Motivating staff and delivering feedback

Being able to rely on your employees to do what you've agreed is essential. Forging a sense of trust remotely will help keep staff motivated to do their part, but there will also be times when things don't go to plan and you need to offer constructive criticism.

Assessing your start point

Managing remotely is easier if you're overseeing an established team that you've already worked with in person. Although you may experience some challenges, you can draw on existing relationships to make it work. Leading a new team remotely is more challenging. They may not know you, and they may not know each other. Forging a sense of trust from a distance comes down to four key areas: communication, recognition, visibility, and vision.

> Whether professionals have a chance to **develop intuitive expertise** depends essentially on the **quality and speed of feedback**

Communication: talk and listen

Regular check-ins are key for **building trust**. Some people will be happy in their own space, but others might feel isolated, which can drain motivation. Checking in isn't micro-management – the goal is to **help staff members feel heard**. Agree how often they'd like to catch up and focus on what they need from you.

Recognition: give credit where it's due

Call out success stories and celebrate "wins" remotely, just as you would in person. Set aside time to **highlight both individual and shared achievements**. It is especially important to recognize **work that goes unnoticed but is fundamental** to an organization's success.

Visibility: give criticism, but be open to it too

Managers are often advised to soften criticism by "sandwiching" it with positive feedback, but staff members are likely to be wise to this approach. Delivering criticism is tricky, but working remotely makes **clarity more important than ever**, and so a more direct style may be more effective. Criticism isn't a personal attack, whichever way it's flowing, but about how a role needs to be executed. Any positive feedback should be about **"course correction"** – realigning the individual's performance with their objectives. Your staff also need to feel empowered to give you feedback, including criticism, so **be open and receptive**.

Vision: invest in their skills

If remote working is a permanent arrangement, you need a **strong vision** of how it will work, and must share it clearly with your staff. Setting up training shows a commitment to your vision and **a willingness to invest in employees**. You can do this remotely through online platforms such as Udemy, Skillshare, and LinkedIn Learning. Don't just be prescriptive – ask staff members what they'd like to learn.

92%

of employees agree that, **if delivered appropriately**, negative feedback is good at improving performance

Creating a thriving team culture

Building a healthy team culture is about blending the professional with the personal. As well as making sure staff share the company's vision and values, managers also need to find ways to get them exchanging ideas, sharing interests, and getting to know each other.

Reinforcing shared values

While you and your staff may not be physically in the same place, you're all striving for the same things. Working remotely makes it easy to focus on differences rather than common threads, so it's important to ensure everyone is aligned to your organization's values. Giving recognition or awards to staff who demonstrate those values is often more motivating than simply repeating them without context.

Giving credit where it's due

If staff have large-scale achievements to highlight, schedule fortnightly "show and tell" sessions, handing the reins to those in question. But it's not all about big objectives: projects often live or die by the small, timely actions that keep

> **Tip**
>
> **PATCH UP**
> Try using **"mission patches"** to celebrate successes. Inspired by NASA, these **physical stickers are designed by staff** to put on their laptops in order to mark a project they worked on.

everyone on course. While these might not warrant a mention in a meeting, a personal thank-you goes a long way.

Letting others lead

Managing remotely can feel like a process of constant delegation. Help yourself and your staff by giving them a role in driving the team forward. Mentoring is a great way to do this for two reasons. Firstly, giving people the chance to contribute to shaping the team in line with a shared vision fosters a sense of ownership. Secondly, pairing a new recruit with an employee invested in the business and who understands how the team works can help get them up to speed quickly, while providing someone to raise concerns with.

> Take time to **recognize the small actions** that help reach shared goals

Case study

GETTING FEEDBACK
Chinese e-commerce giant Alibaba.com has embraced remote working, even going so far as to build its own tools, such as the productivity and messaging app DingTalk, which it uses to deliver weekly training sessions and lectures.

The organization has also united its drive for efficiency with a forum for letting staff voice their opinions. Like many other companies, Alibaba.com is keen to make sure staff meetings are worthwhile, and don't get in the way of the work itself. In every meeting, one member of staff is assigned to track time, while other attendees rate the meeting's usefulness. In this way staff can deliver instant feedback and share and comment on their experiences with a view to improving future meetings.

Maintaining authority from a distance

Leadership and authority go hand in hand: you can't manage effectively unless you can control the direction of your staff. Maintaining authority can be harder when you're only in touch remotely, but by earning trust and remaining focused, you'll keep your staff on your side.

Exercising authority

Exercising authority in the workplace is not about cracking the whip and imposing your will, it's about staying in control of your team's direction. Good leaders inspire others to do their best work, but they also keep people engaged and focused on their goals. This is harder when everyone is working from their own space and you're relying on remote communication to stay in control.

Earning respect

Understanding your staff's personalities and getting them to regard you as their leader is essential. Achieving this requires a blend of building trust and showing decisiveness. Keep in mind that respect is earned, not demanded. If your organization is undergoing changes, you might feel sugar-coating news is kinder, but giving people the straight truth is likely to win you greater respect. While it's important to hear your employees' thoughts on what works and what doesn't, remember that you're the one making the final decisions. That doesn't mean laying down rules for the sake of it, but it does mean setting out a clear vision and making choices that advance everyone towards it.

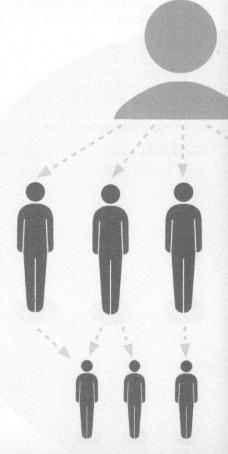

Understand what's happening

When you have individuals or small teams focusing on their own tasks and working alone it can lead to other parts of the organization not knowing what's going on or, worse, duplicating work. This problem is likely to be more pronounced in remote teams. As a leader, it's up to you to give direction, but you can only do that if you know what's happening. During daily team calls, ask people for a quick update on what they did yesterday and what they're planning today.

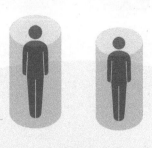

In focus

KEEPING STAFF MEMBERS ENGAGED

Engagement, focus, and structure are essential in every work place, wherever it happens to be. The challenges of remote working can easily become a distraction, so it's important to keep your employees motivated and focused on what matters most. Set definite goals for both the near and long term, and make sure you communicate them clearly so your staff understand their overarching direction and objectives.

Index

Acknowledgments

Quotes and stats

p.10 IWG Global Workspace Survey 2019

p.15 Dan Lucy, *Financial Times* 28 November 2020

p.25 The imposter phenomenon in high achieving women: Dynamics and therapeutic intervention, Pauline Rose Clance & Suzanne Imes, 1978

p.27 IES Working at Home Wellbeing survey April 2020

p.30 www.pwc.com/us/en/services/consulting/library/consumer-intelligence-series/tech-at-work.html#insight6

p.31 *The Social CEO: How Social Media Can Make You A Stronger Leader*, Damian Corbet, 2019

p.34 slack.com/intl/en-es/blog/news/slack-announces-record-first-quarter-fiscal-year-2021-results

p.44 Varonis 2019 Global Data Risk Report

p.60 Gianpiero Petriglieri, *Financial Times*, 14 May 2020

p.65 www.markletic.com/blog/virtual-event-statistics/

p.72 *The Long-Distance Leader: Rules for Remarkable Remote Leadership*, Kevin Eikenberry and Wayne Turmel, 2018

p.76 Igloo Software, State of the Digital Workplace report

p.79 OneLogin, State of Remote Work survey report 2020

p.80 Gartner 2020 poll of 334 HR leaders

p.85 Gartner, Changing Change Management report 2019

The Contagious Leader, Journal of Applied Psychology 2005

p.87 LinkedIn's 2019 "Workplace Learning Report" survey

p.88 *Thinking, Fast and Slow*, Daniel Kahneman, 2012

p.89 Jack Zenger and Joseph Folkman, *Harvard Business Review*, 15 January 2014

Authors' acknowledgments

Thanks to Matthew Fox, Jules Machajski, Carrie Brophy, Daniel Gill and Giacomo Kavanagh for their help with elements of this book. Thanks to Claire Lister at Dynamo for the opportunity, Nick Funnell for being our editor and everyone at DK for pulling it all together.

Publisher's acknowledgments

The publisher would like to thank Claire Lister, Kate Ford, and Andrew Fishleigh at Dynamo for producing this edition. Also, Jean Coppendale for proofreading and David Ballheimer for indexing. The publisher would also like to thank Balwant Singh and Bimlesh Tiwary for their technical support.

First edition produced for Dorling Kindersley Limited by Dynamo Ltd